The Journey *of* BECOMING

GURNOOR KAUR SETHI

BlueRose ONE.com
Stories Matter
NewDelhi • London

BLUEROSE PUBLISHERS
India | U.K.

For permissions requests or inquiries regarding this publication,
please contact:

BLUEROSE PUBLISHERS
www.BlueRoseONE.com
info@bluerosepublishers.com
+91 8882 898 898
+4407342408967

ISBN: 978-93-7542-404-8

Cover design: Daksh
Typesetting: Tanya Raj Upadhyay

First Edition: January 2026

To my parents, thank you for being both my roots and my wings, teaching me how to love and how to let go.

To my sister, thank you for being my biggest supporter through thick and thin.

To the reader, thank you for letting my words reach out and sit beside your thoughts.

PREFACE

This book is a poetic examination of how we deal with love, loss, self-doubt, joy, and growth while coming to see ourselves more kindly and clearly. There are moments when life feels like a puzzle whose pieces keep changing shape.

These poems are my way of keeping the chaos together and turning it into something beautiful. These poems have the truths that I learned only after they broke me. Whenever I am lost in the grey, I tend to play with words and put out all my emotions.

I hope these words will be a reminder to you that there is beauty in uncertainty too.

It's more than just a book.

You can enter this peaceful space whenever the outside world becomes too noisy.

It's the answers you've been holding inside and the questions you've been scared to ask.

Pieces of me can be found in these pages, whether they are in love, grief, laughter, or the in-between.

I pieced together some of these words from my personal experiences.

Some may feel as though they were written specifically for you, and in a sense, they were.

When you feel light in the morning and heavy at night, this book is for you.

For the sunrises you have yet to see and the storms you have weathered, these words are for you.

Table of Contents

BLOOM

I see the sunshine falling down on a quiet morning
Like a love letter from the universe
The world shines, all bright and cheer
Feels like everything I want is clear
And for a moment
I believe all I need is near.

I felt a shift, a change
but the sky was still the same
The first greet, the first hello
wasn't so grand, but a gentle mellow
Your laughter mingled with the breeze,
A melody that brought me ease.

I always come home to the warmth
of love and tenderness
I come home to myself
To my safe place, to the place that gives me comfort
It is what is taught
To love but with self-first.

Something feels different
Might have been the coffee or the weather
But all I knew, it was my heart
floating towards your soul like a feather.
Each glance a thread, each word a seam,
We spun a tapestry, a waking dream.

I spent years chasing ‘one day’
hoping someone would cross my way
With every step, the shadows grew bright
A dance of fate under the moonlight
I chose to follow, to flow with it,
wondering about all the possibilities, I sit

There were things I realized and stuff I had no answer to

Yet, my heart followed the path to you.

I gather the pieces, both lost and found

In this journey, our hearts beat profound

With every heartbeat, the future unfurls

Two souls awakening to new worlds.

Love, a simple word
With a long definition
“What is love?” they ask
Love is when you start believing in magic
Love is when you stare at the moon
Love is what makes you believe again
Love is what makes your sorrow drain
Love is when you find ways to talk to them
Love is when you are far but not apart
Love is when you give it a chance
Love makes you sway like you dance
Love is what can be seen in your eyes
Love is when you realize
“Oh oh, I’m falling in love!!”

I spend moments laughing
with the people whom I barely know
But I've started to like it
because that's how you grow
I never really thought of
making new friends
But at this moment
I feel like I might go with the trend
To share the gossip, the story about me
for in their laughter, I find my own glee.

I never imagined this joy could unfold

As laughter and stories start weaving a gold

So here's to the moments, both silly and true

In the arms of the unknown, I've found something new.

Love isn’t always grand

it might be just a glance

Sometimes it’s the right words, the right action

Maybe not the right time but the right intention.

It’s when I told my friends about you

that my little crush turned into something true.

Let our hearts be the only sound
Let the laughs grow all around
Cause I've told the stars about you
Cause I'm falling in love with you
Cause I want to know more about you
Cause I've started to like all about you
Cause I see the way you look at me
Oh, I know you've started to care about me.

In the quiet moments, in the simple sighs

In the warmth of the night beneath soft, lingering skies

With every heartbeat echoing clear

Love isn't a race, it's the path that we steer

So let's write our story, in ink made of dreams

A tapestry woven from laughter and themes

In this dance of the heart, let's take our chance

Finding solace and joy in this sweet romance.

My life has become very new
With people surrounding me
People whom I trust
People who now know a lot
Was it foolish to open up so wide?
Yet here we are, with nothing left to hide
Growing up has its own perks
It's on you how you make it up
Embracing the journey, however it turns
For in these connections, a bright fire burns.

You remember everything
From my favourites to my hates
You promise never to break my heart
Destiny cannot keep us apart
It's always about the right person
Who will wait for the right time
AND YOU SAY YOU WILL.
FOREVER?
There are certain things unspoken
But it all goes past smooth
I know you know it all
You understand
Do I need to speak it out loud for you to hear?
Maybe not, because you are always near
And that's what binds us together
And together we dream of forever.

I am not the same as I was before
Life has broken me open to this beautiful reality
of love, of friendship, of trust
I just want this to stay as a whole for life.

CLOUDS

They still laugh with me

And your eyes still find mine

My heart still flutters when he says my name

But amidst all

A cloud drifts in

Making me feel as if it knows something that I don't.

The evenings don’t feel the same
Something lies in between us
Unsaid, Unwanted
Your replies are getting shorter
One word. When you know I hate it
The happiness is left hanging on a thread
But I trust you
You said, “Don’t let me go even if I want to".

Friends pass by with smiles
Some feel like waving from across the river
There is no stopping by to wait for me
No breaks to spill the tea
Echoes of laughter linger, but fade to a whisper
I reach for the warmth, but find only a shiver

You still talk to me
Still smile but not at me
Nothing stays in the air or touches my heart
I can't help but notice that something's broken
Oh dear heart!

Many voices echo in the room
But the one I want to hear is missing
This feeling of emptiness settles in my heart
Why is the destiny testing?

For days, I look around to see the face
That I have adored for long
Because I knew you would stay
But you proved me wrong
Each laugh now feels like a foreign song
As shadows lengthen, time drags on
Memories, like whispers, dance through the night
Leaving me aching for lost light.

STORM

the tears fall down,
unknown of the reason
i wipe them out.
i sit back and ponder,
when i realise
the approaching thunder.
it feels so heavy,
like a pierce in my heart
i want to go back,
go again to the start.
why must the clouds gather,
and drown the hope in me?
with every drop that falls,
i yearn to set it free.

The old times,
The times when we laughed.
We shared and we cared.
Bounded but tried.
Oh how we fell,
Fell into a well of love.
How one eye contact was enough for us,
Little excuses to pass each other around.
Oh how we thought about it forever.

Look at us now,

I don't know how things went wrong,

But I am here to talk.

Here to take things back in time.

Making things right.

I am waiting, even if it doesn’t matter to you.

I won’t let you go even if you want to now.

Oh just give us a chance. Once and for all.

Is it my mistake that I love?

I love but not say

Is it my mistake that I care?

Care with all my heart not just for sake

Is it my mistake that I believe?

Believe that they know me

Is it my mistake that I trust?

Trust that their words won't hurt me

Am I that bad?
That bad, to be treated like that
Treated like I don't matter
Is that what I am?
A burden to be done
Done for the sake of god
I know I am not the best
But am I that worst, to be called like that
Called like I am waste, waste of time

I try, try everyday

Try to be better, to be best

But i fail, I fail every single time

Am I that bad?

That bad, that no one understands me?

Understand to see how hurt I am

How torn I am!

Oh, sorry, I don't GET hurt cause I GIVE hurt!

I think I am that bad

That bad to just left to be broken!

ROOTS

Growing up is a mystery, I can bid
Expectations are what just only build
Complicated things all at once
Pressure comes all in tons
Misunderstood is what you are
The way sugar seems like salt in a jar
Breaking apart, nothing you can do
The mind is buzzing like a zoo
Right seems wrong, wrong seems right
Just someone to lead the path I must find
Standing in a storm I stay low
With no more courage I wish to let go.

I write to you all what's unsaid
My heart pours through its dead end
Sitting on my bed, I see our frame
I was so in love but for you it was lame.

A canvas now empty where we used to reside
Silence stretches its arms so wide
Whispers of laughter in those past days
Now unknown, but familiar in many ways.
I never think of sending you the letter
As I now I don't want to make it better
From my heart, my forever, my dream
Today I break you free.

Life is a lie, a lie so true,
That you believe once you go through.
Oh I wonder how do I exist,
Then comes a vision buried in mist.
What's real?, what's not?
Thinking about it, our minds rot.
What to believe? What to leave?
There are things I never would perceive.

It is a web of perplexion that goes deep,
You see people in a corner, they weep.
Some faces glow in the dark,
The way they unfurl their spark.

How can I be them? Why am I me?
A question to be answered, all plea.
In the silence, I hear the unheard,
Echoes of thoughts, a restless bird.

Living Through It All

Longing for love, easy to hate,
I ponder sitting out too late.
They say “Believe in the trust you built”,
Then why? Why does it break with guilt?
Advices are what so easy to say,
Hard to follow when the path turns grey.
Every step feels unsure, yet I move anyway.

The glitter surely all seems gold,
But the reality beneath them is still untold.
A day will come, when you unfold,
Your life is a miracle, your spirit behold.

I stand in a crowd thinking what is the need
To speak your heart or to do the deed
Just stay mum and press it down your throat
No one will listen to your random note
You might care about what they think
And one day everything will change in an eye blink

You will notice the change in You whole
Oppression of the dark, suppression of the soul
Blurred vision on a negative way
If you want to escape then you not may
Before this all could happen you need to think,
To save your boat from the deep sink.

RISE

The world is full of chaos
Where I find silence all times
Hidden somewhere in a corner
Waiting for me to arrive there
I know once I reach I won't come back
But still I want to explore all the ends

Tired of this hustle in the veins I want to soar like a free broken leaf

The end is near but the freedom is ensured

The decision is mixed but the intention is pure

The line of life is never straight

You never know which turn it takes.

Beneath that mask is a girl who wished a lot
The girl who once cried her eyes out
That girl who didn’t know the word NO
Oh! What a people pleaser she is, they said

The mask is where she has hidden herself

Scared of this scarred world she might drown in

She chose to be separated, separated from the dwelling

Oh! What a miser she is, they said

Miser, Loser, Pleaser is what they only know
Unaware of the torment she was into
Laugh is only what they do
Because they have never been in her shoe
With each step forward, she sheds the old skin,
Embracing her flaws, letting the healing begin.

Believe in yourself
Love with yourself
The hurt will pass
But if you keep holding on
You will shatter like a broken glass.

See the beauty the world holds
Stop searching the answers for the untold
Mistakes are what show the reality
Reality, that's buried so deep in your heart
To reach there you must plough
And then you will find,
Every mistake is what made you grow

WINGS

I have decided to stop waiting for closure
I let the wind carry my guilt
I choose to water my own garden
Stand high with the strength I built

I see the beauty of imperfection
Of uncompleted things
I've started to enjoy my own company
The magic of slow mornings.
A cup of my favourite coffee
with my forever people
MY FAMILY.

Strange right? How after every broken heart
And every tragedy
When we turn back
We always find our family
Waiting upon our return
To their embrace and shadow
Where love is abundant
Worries narrow.

I've learnt to spread my wings
Take a high leap
Away from the willows of my heart
Now only bliss I reap.

I am not who I was yesterday
Nor fully my future self I became
I change and reshape
As I've experienced life's game.

Each of my scar blooms into a story
I shed old skins
Step out of the cages unseen
The world says "arrive",
but I whisper back
"I am not meant for endings,
I am forever becoming".